Armstrong

Song Album 1

for low/medium voice
with piano accompaniment

Cecil Armstrong Gibbs (1889-1960) studied music and history at Trinity College, Cambridge. Whilst there, he met Edward J. Dent, Charles Wood, Vaughan Williams and the singer Steuart Wilson. From 1915 he taught history, classics and English at The Wick School, Hove, the preparatory school he had attended as a boy. The turning event of his life came in 1919. He wanted a school play to celebrate the headmaster's retirement, and wrote to Walter de la Mare. The result was the play *Crossings*, written by de la Mare, produced by E. J. Dent and J. B. Trend, and with music by Gibbs conducted by Adrian Boult. Boult was so impressed by the songs that he persuaded Gibbs to study at the Royal College of Music with Vaughan Williams and Charles Wood. In 1921 Gibbs joined the staff of the Royal College, and in 1923 began a long career as an adjudicator at music festivals.

Gibbs composed a prolific amount of practical music for amateur choirs and orchestras, always skilfully written; such music was immensely useful if not always memorable. He wrote three symphonies and a choral symphony, *Odysseus*, which, but for the outbreak of war, would have been premiered in November 1939. However, it is for his songs that he will be remembered. Some 150 songs were published during his lifetime. Some of these, such as *Five Eyes*, *Silver* and *The Fields are Full* are so familiar that they have become almost hackneyed. Unfortunately, many singers continue to perform the few well-known songs and fail to explore any of the rest of the composer's work. The purpose of anthologies, in music as in poetry, is to stimulate an interest in the work of chosen writers. For several years it has been difficult for singers to explore Gibbs's output, as the majority of his songs have been out of print. The publication of two volumes, containing almost all the songs which were published by Curwen, means that over a third of his output is easily available again.

Nine of the songs in this volume are settings of poems by de la Mare. In 1951 Herbert Howells wrote to Gibbs: 'You've never yet failed in *any* setting you've done of beloved Jack de la Mare's poems', and the songs here show the aptness of Howells's comment. The earliest of these are the three songs from *Crossings*, originally written with accompaniment for flute, three violins, viola, cello and piano; a piano accompaniment was published with the play in 1921, and the songs published separately in 1924. *Beggar's Song* is straightforwardly cheerful. *Araby* and *Ann's Cradle Song* appear simple and were written to be sung by a child. However they still manage, by deft harmonic touches in the accompaniment, to convey something of de la Mare's feeling for the mysterious. *Lullaby* has most attractive contrasts between major and minor within the soothing flow of quavers. *The Sleeping Beauty* is purely atmospheric, whilst presenting two pictures, the motionless sleeping beauty herself, and the almost invisible moths and crickets surrounding her. *The Scarecrow* is an excitingly dramatic setting of de la Mare's imaginative description of the life of a scarecrow. *The Wanderer* and *The Galliass* are two more of Gibbs's deceptively simple songs, which grow more interesting with every hearing. *The Mad Prince* contains in its first line the words *Peacock Pie* which was the title of de la Mare's famous volume of children's verse, which not only inspired Gibbs, but also Herbert Howells and Lennox Berkeley. It is only near the end that it becomes clear that the prince has lost his reason through the death of his beloved, and Gibbs's high ostinato for the central section portrays this sense of loss well.

John Masefield's *By a Bier-Side* comes from his play *The Tragedy of Pompey the Great*, published in 1915, and the words were spoken by the 'The Chief Centurions' over the dead body of Pompey. When the poem was published in *Complete Poems* in 1923, some of the words were altered; in particular the first phrase became 'Man is a sacred city', which enables the poem to stand alone. Presumably the composer did not know this revised version of the poem. This is one of Gibbs's finest songs, bold and dignified in the face of death. The two Irish songs, *The Market* and *Padraic the Fidiler* are both dance-like numbers, though the first ends with a cheerful curse, and the second with regret. The latter has an optional violin obbligato. *Danger*, a setting of words by Gibbs's friend Sir Mordaunt Currie, has a moto perpetuo accompaniment rather like that of *The Beggar's Song*, but with more elaborate harmonic progressions. The slightly sentimental religious words of *The Tiger-Lily* are saved from mawkishness by Gibbs's understated chromatic touches of harmony. *The Cherry Tree* has words by Margaret Rose, who provided texts for some well-known songs by Michael Head. The music is utterly charming, and ends with a moving cadence in the realisation that the beloved will never return.

Michael Pilkington

Cover photo:
Royal College of Music,
London.

Exclusive distributors:
Music Sales Limited,
Newmarket Road,
Bury St. Edmunds,
Suffolk IP33 3YB.

Order No. NOV170363
ISBN 0-85360-909-8

This compilation
© Copyright 1998
Novello & Company Limited,
14/15 Berners Street,
London W1T 3LJ.
All rights reserved.

Book design by
Michael Bell Design.
Printed in the United Kingdom.

No part of this publication may be copied or reproduced in any form or by any means without the prior permission of Novello Publishing Limited.

Ann's Cradle Song 22

Araby 28

Beggar's Song 32

By a Bier-Side 39

The Cherry Tree 57

Danger 58

The Galliass 42

Lullaby 4

The Mad Prince 14

The Market 50

Padraic the Fidiler 63

The Scarecrow 9

The Sleeping Beauty 18

The Tiger-Lily 46

The Wanderer 54

Lullaby

Words by Walter de la Mare
Music by Armstrong Gibbs

The Scarecrow

Words by Walter de la Mare
Music by Armstrong Gibbs

Music copyright © 1931 Armstrong Gibbs; exclusively licensed to J. Curwen & Sons Ltd. Words reproduced by permission.

The Mad Prince

Words by Walter de la Mare
Music by Armstrong Gibbs

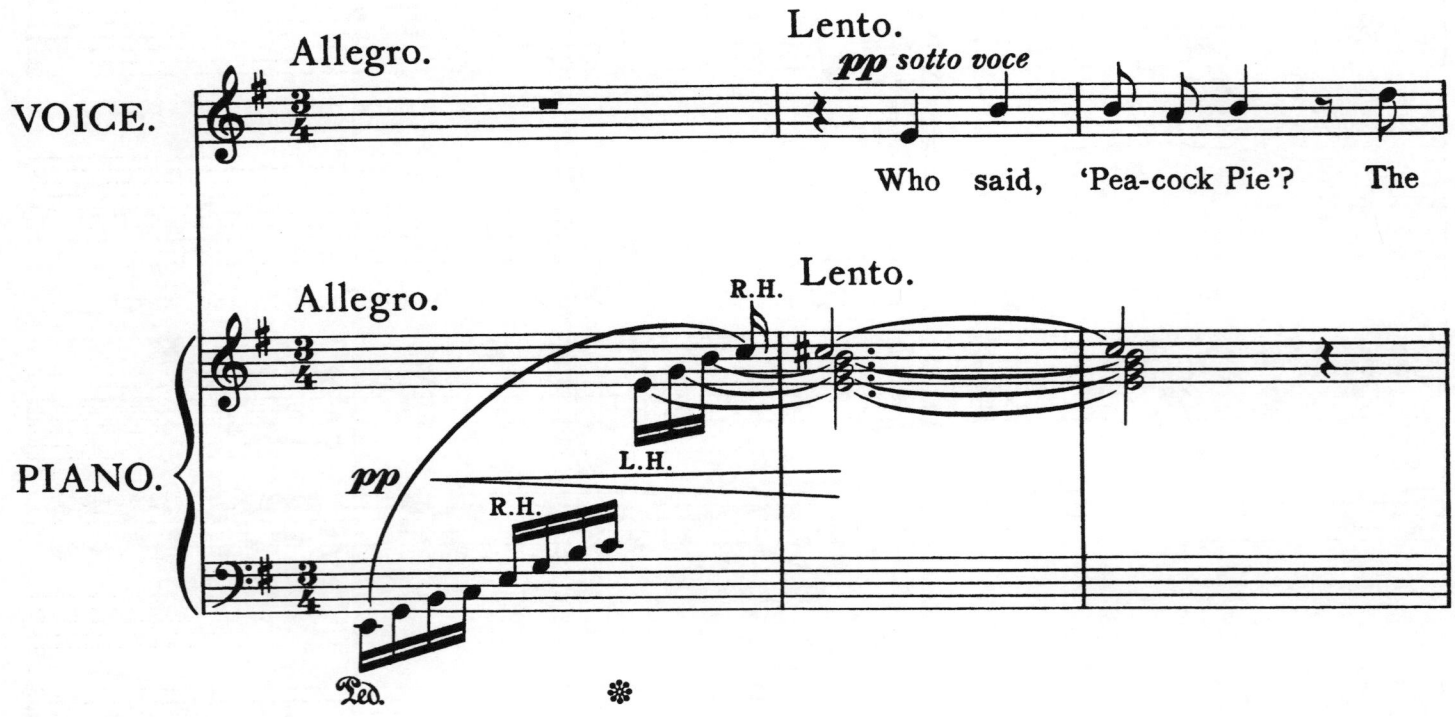

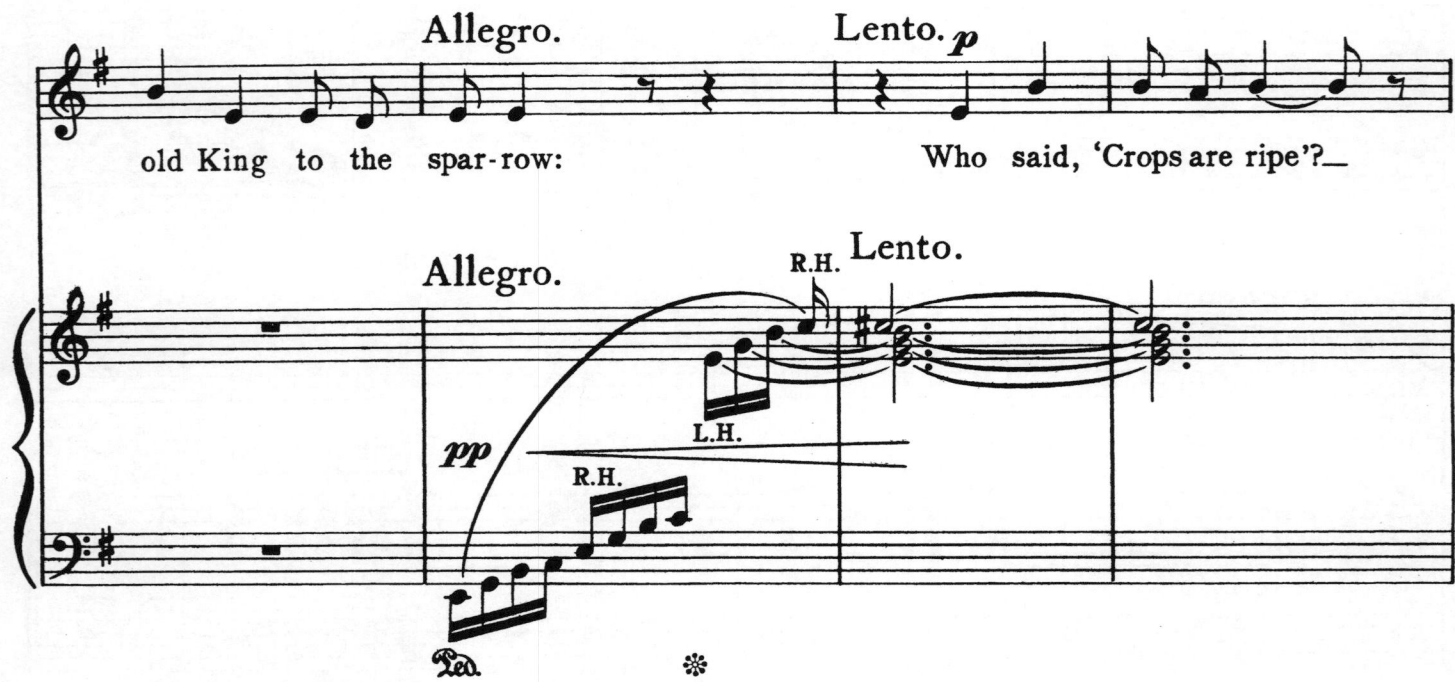

Music copyright © 1922 Armstrong Gibbs; exclusively licensed to J. Curwen & Sons Ltd. Words reproduced by permission.

The Sleeping Beauty

Words by Walter de la Mare
Music by Armstrong Gibbs

Music copyright © 1924 Armstrong Gibbs; exclusively licensed to J. Curwen & Sons Ltd. Words reproduced by permission.

Ann's Cradle Song

Sallie's Song from the play *Crossings*
Words by Walter de la Mare
Music by Armstrong Gibbs

Music copyright © 1924 Armstrong Gibbs; exclusively licensed to J. Curwen & Sons Ltd. Words reproduced by permission.

Araby

Sallie's Song from the play *Crossings*
Words by Walter de la Mare
Music by Armstrong Gibbs

Music copyright © 1924 Armstrong Gibbs; exclusively licensed to J. Curwen & Sons Ltd. Words reproduced by permission.

Beggar's Song

from the play *Crossings*
Words by Walter de la Mare
Music by Armstrong Gibbs

Music copyright © 1924 Armstrong Gibbs; exclusively licensed to J. Curwen & Sons Ltd. Words reproduced by permission.

Soon Moll and Nan in dreams are laid, And snoring Dick's a-sleep; Then still,_____ O; dale and hill,_____

O;_____ Snow's_____ fall'n_____ deep._____

By a Bier-Side

Words by John Masefield
from *The Tragedy of Pompey the Great*
Music by Armstrong Gibbs

Beau-ty was in this brain and in this ea - ger hand:

Death is so blind and dumb Death does not un - der - stand.—

Death drifts the brain with dust and soils the young limbs' glo - ry,

Death makes jus-tice a dream, and strength a tra-vel-ler's sto - ry.

Death drives the lovely soul to wander under the sky.

Death o-pens un-known doors — It is most grand to die.

To Marjorie Leaster Dixon

The Galliass

Words by Walter de la Mare
Music by Armstrong Gibbs

Andante legatissimo.

'Tell me, tell me, Un-known strang-er, When shall I sight me That tall ship

Music copyright © 1924 Armstrong Gibbs; exclusively licensed to J. Curwen & Sons Ltd. Words reproduced by permission.

On whose flower-wreathed coun-ter is gild-ed *Sleep?*'

'Lands-man, lands-man, Lynx nor kes-trel Ne'er shall des-cry from O-cean steep That mid-night steal-ing, high-poop'd gal-liass, *Sleep.'*

'Pro-mise me, Strang-er, Though I mark not When cold night-tide's

Shad-ows creep *Thou* wilt keep un-wa-ve-ring watch for *Sleep.'*

'Myr-iad the lights are, Way-worn lands-man, Rock-ing the dark through On the deep: She a-lone burns none to prove her Sleep.'

45

The Tiger-Lily

Words by Dorothy Pleydell Bouverie
Music by Armstrong Gibbs

Lento con dolore.

At night in black Geth-sem-an-e Our Lord was pray-ing there. The flow'rs all

Music copyright © 1924 Armstrong Gibbs; exclusively licensed to J. Curwen & Sons Ltd. Words reproduced by permission.

bowed their heads— and wept His grief they fain— would share—

A-lone there stood in robes of gold The ti-ger-lil - y vain. No tear-drops would this flow-er shed For her dear Mas - ter's pain.—

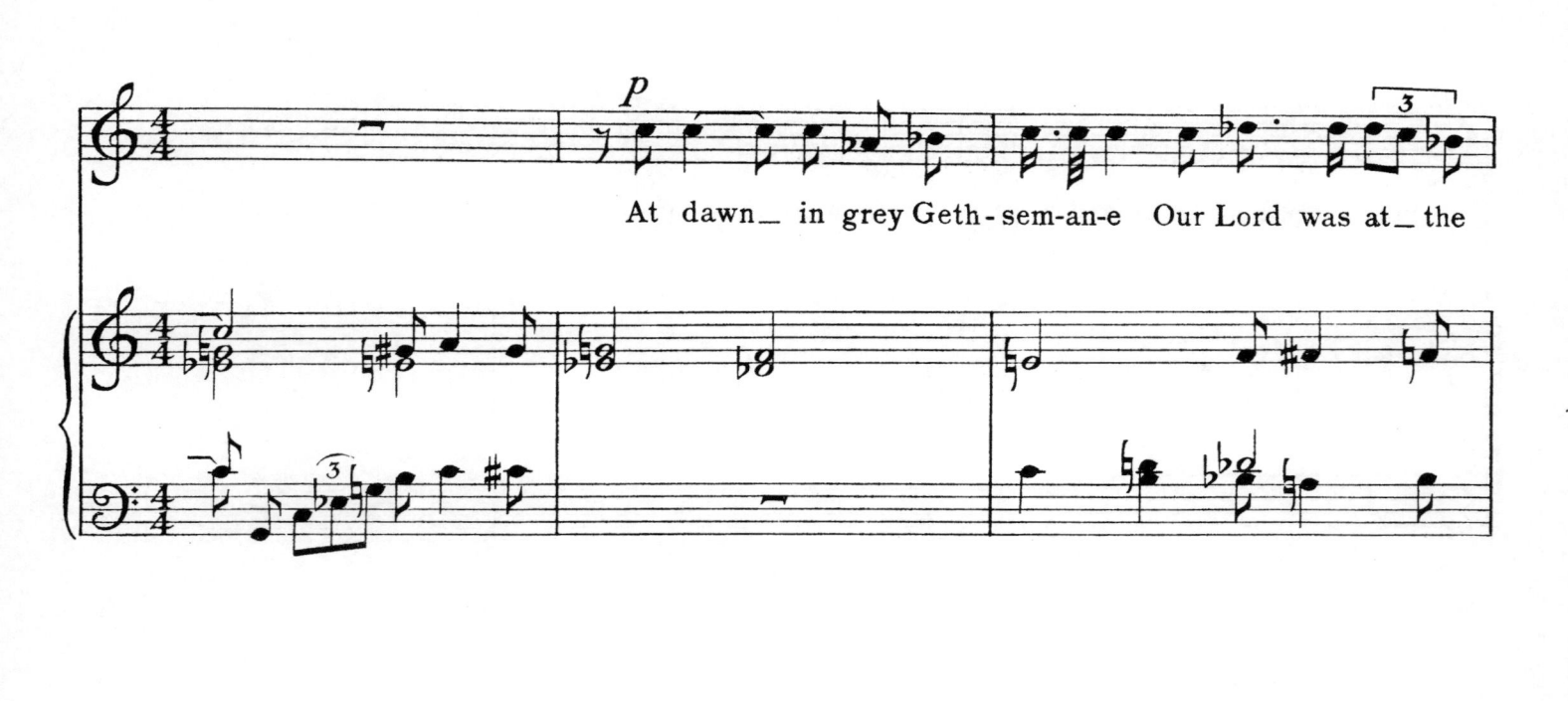

At dawn in grey Gethsemane Our Lord was at the gate; His gaze fell on this lily cold, Then turned to meet His fate.

In dew dis-solved the flower's pride And ev-er down the years

With-in her pet-als still a-bide Her own im-mort-al tears.

Danbury 1921.

The Market

Words by James Stephens
Music by Armstrong Gibbs

Allegro con fuoco.

A man came to me at the fair And said,— "If you've a po-et's tongue, Tum-ble up and chant the air____ That the stars of morn-ing sung."

Music copyright © 1926 Armstrong Gibbs; exclusively licensed to J. Curwen & Sons Ltd. Words reproduced by permission.

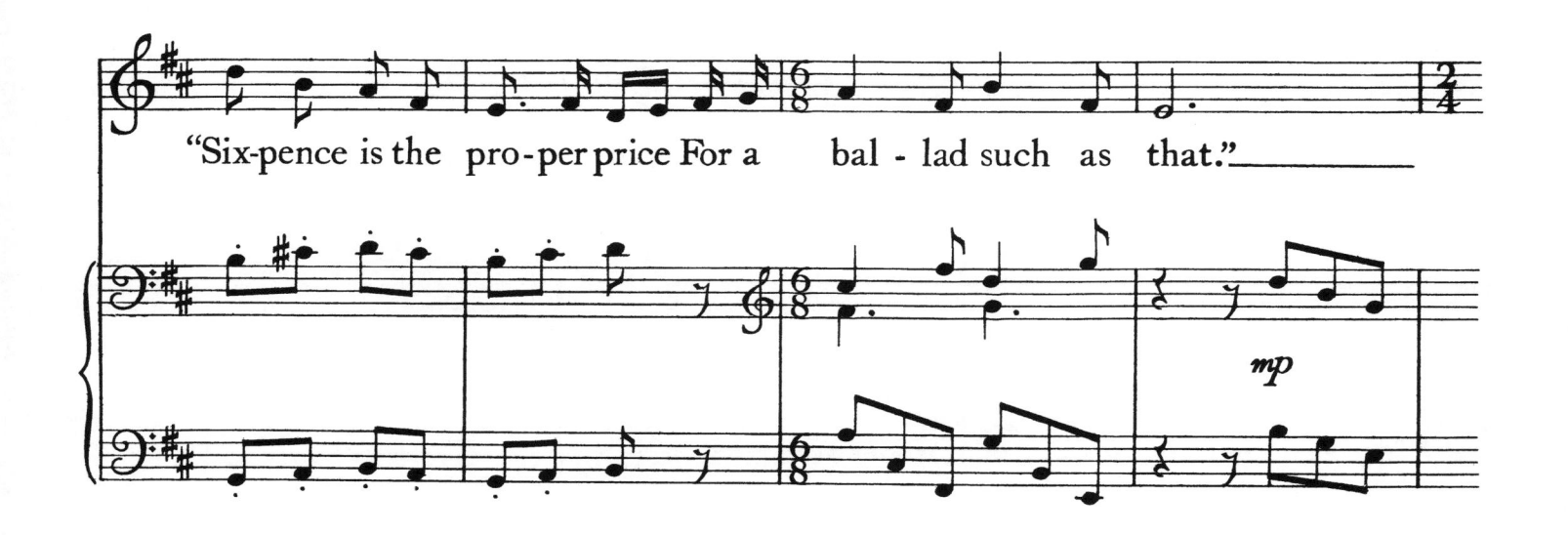

"I'll pay you, if you sing it nice, A penny piece." I answered flat, "Sixpence is the proper price For a ballad such as that."

But he stared___ and wagged his head,

Growl-ing as he passed a-long,

"Six-pence! well, I'll see you dead___ Before I pay that for a song."

I saw him buy three pints of stout With the six-pence— dir-ty lout!

53

The Wanderer

Words by Walter de la Mare
Music by Armstrong Gibbs

Will he ever be weary of wandering, The flaming sun? Ever weary of waning in love-light, The white still moon?

Music copyright © 1926 Armstrong Gibbs; exclusively licensed to J. Curwen & Sons Ltd. Words reproduced by permission.

Will ever a shepherd come With a crook of simple gold, And lead all the little stars like lambs to the fold? Will ev - er the wan-der-er sail From o - ver the sea,

Up the riv - er of wa-ter, To the stones to me?

Will he take us all in - to his ship,

p *poco a poco cresc.*

Dream - ing, and waft us far,

To where in the clouds of the west The is - lands

are?

Danger

Words by Mordaunt Currie
from *Discoveries and Dreams*
Music by Armstrong Gibbs

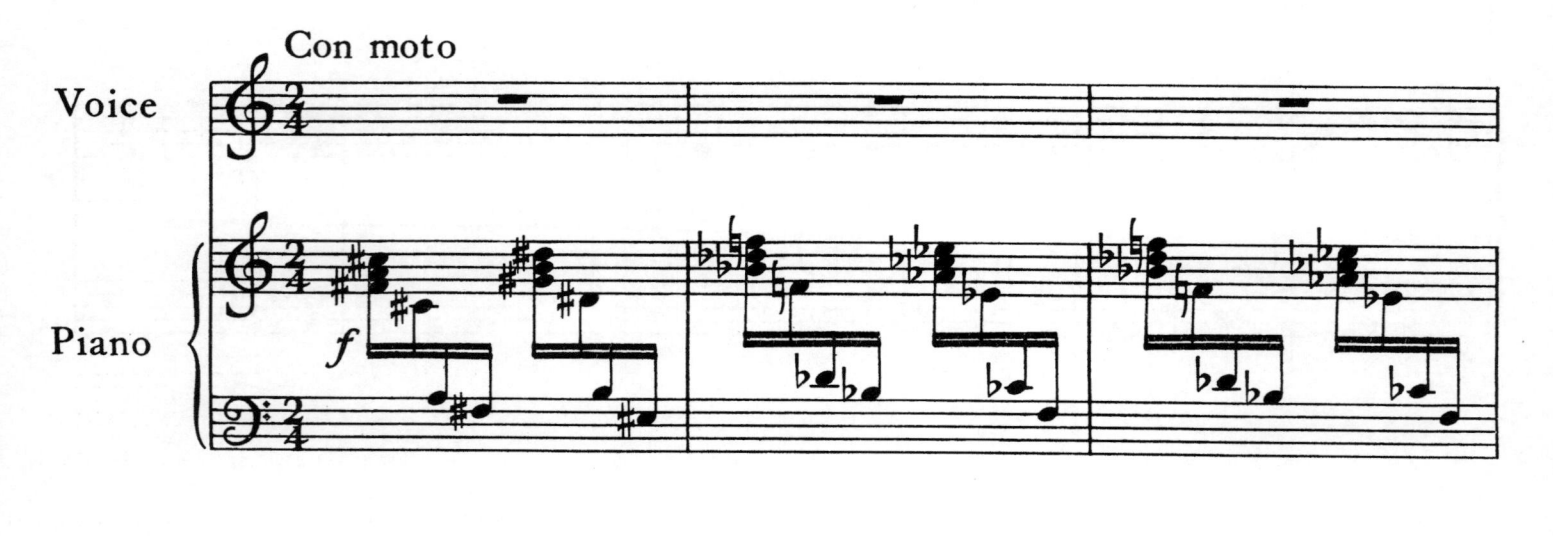

You shall not go a-may-ing when the thorn is white once more, For still the Goat-Foot wan-ders in the haunts he lov'd be-

-fore. You shall not go a-may-ing, lest per-chance at close of day The Un-nam'd come soft-foot-ed for to steal my love a-way.

You shall not go a-walking in the twi-light by the stream, Lest river-gods should mark you, with your gold-en hair a-gleam, And pray'rs be un-a-vail-ing and the wa-ter-lil-ies fair Should cov-er up your beau-ty and the reeds mock my despair.

You shall not go a-wandering when all the stars are bright, Lest some Hero of the Heavens should lean out from the night And clasp you close and bear you to the shin-ing fields a-

-far To look down on my sor-row with the

bright eyes of a star.

Padraic the Fidiler

Words by Padraic Gregory
Music by Armstrong Gibbs

Poco allegretto

Pad - raic sits in the gar - den In - un-der the bright new moon,⎯⎯⎯ And from his

N.B: If a violin be available, the passages lying between the marks ❊⎯❊ may be played upon it, the piano taking the rest of the harmony.
The violin obbligato starts at the first note of the introduction.

Music copyright © 1931 Armstrong Gibbs; exclusively licensed to J. Curwen & Sons Ltd. Words reproduced by permission.

fid - il coax-es A love - - ly dream - y tune.

Och! I love the tune he's play - in' An' I wisht it was for me; But I know it's for the bird - eens Up in the cher - ry tree.

Shure iv-er-y night they peep from In-un-der their moth-er's wings.

Tae hear the sil-v'ry mu-sic His wee dark fid-il sings.

An' for them he's al - ways play - in' An' has-nae a thought for me; For if I go out he wand - hers A-way from the cher - ry tree.

The Cherry Tree

Words by Margaret Rose
Music by Armstrong Gibbs

The cherry's a-bloom in the North-land, The wild, lone cher-ry tree.

Music copyright © 1949 Armstrong Gibbs; exclusively licensed to J. Curwen & Sons Ltd. Words reproduced by permission.

The sad, sweet birds of the Spring-time are singing a - gain to me. They sing of the fro - zen riv - ers,

Pi - ping soft and low _____ Till I think I hear _____ your foot - steps danc - ing a - cross the snow.

Sing, birds! Sing songs of the Spring-time, Sing high on the cherry tree.

mf Tempo I
Sing of my love in the North - land ___ As my love once
mf Tempo I
sang to me. ___
pp poco meno mosso
Hush, birds! the cher- ry in si - lence Is
pp sub. poco meno mosso

letting her petals fall ⎯⎯ For one whose dancing footsteps Will never come ⎯⎯ at all. ⎯⎯